BOOK 3: MAKING MUSIC

The Classic Piano Course

Learning to play the piano for older beginners in three easy parts.

CAROL BARRATT

This book © Copyright 1995 Chester Music.
Order No. CH60248. ISBN 0-7119-2993-9.

Chester Music

Preface

Thanks to Leslie East for his help in realizing this project.

Pictures in this book are reproduced by permission of
the Royal College of Music, the Hulton Deutsch Collection Limited, and the Mary Evans Picture Library,
and are credited in captions under each picture.

Music processed by New Notations.
Cover design by Pearce Marchbank.
Cover illustration by Brian Grimwood.

Main Topics covered in Book 2

Range of notes:

The major scale, G major, F major

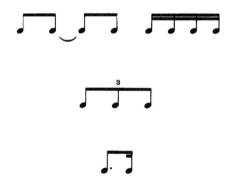

Book 3

CONTENTS

General Topics

Pieces

Sonatina

(Op.36 No.3 – Second movement)

Un poco Adagio

Muzio Clementi (1752-1832)

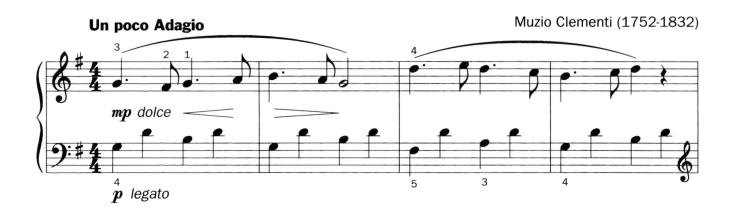

Fascinating snippet

Clementi is often called 'the father of true piano-playing' as he was probably the first composer to write specifically for the piano as opposed to the harpsichord. He knew Beethoven, Mozart and Haydn. Born in Rome, he travelled extensively, eventually returning to live in London in 1810.

Prelude

(Op.28 No.7)

Fascinating snippet

Even Chopin suffered from 'concert' nerves and once stated,
"I am not fitted to give concerts. The audience intimidates me, I feel
choked by its breath, paralysed by its curious glances, struck dumb
by all those strange faces."

Chopin leaving his last concert,
16 November 1848.

Adapted from
Frédéric Chopin (1810-49)

Suggested listening

Listen to other preludes by Chopin. Also to others by
Rakhmaninov and Debussy.

La Donna È Mobile

'Woman is Wayward'

from *Rigoletto*

Fascinating snippet

'M. Verdi is a musician of decadence. He has all its defects, the violence of the style, the incoherence of ideas, the crudity of colours, the impropriety of language.'

(*Revue des Deux Mondes*, Paris, 15 December 1856)

Adapted from
Giuseppe Verdi (1813-1901)

Allegretto

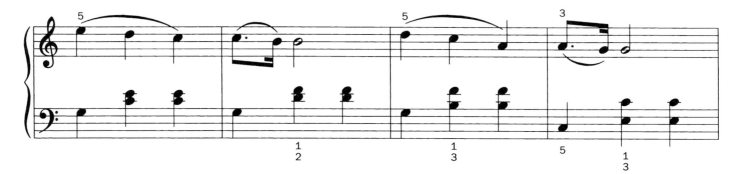

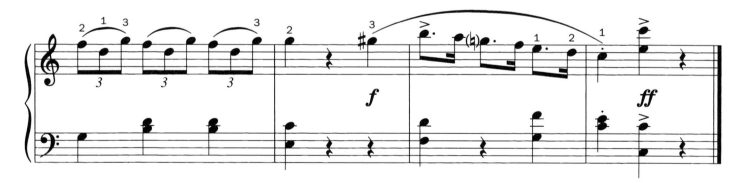

Suggested listening

Listen to this aria in its original form. Also, listen to other operas
by Verdi such as *La Traviata* and *Il Trovatore*.

The minor scale

There is *one* kind of major scale but there are *two* types of minor scale, the *melodic minor* and the *harmonic minor* scale. Melodies in a minor key tend to be based on the melodic version. Chords are usually taken from the harmonic version.

For each major key there is a *relative minor*. Related keys have the same key signature.
A relative minor starts on the 6th note of the major scale.

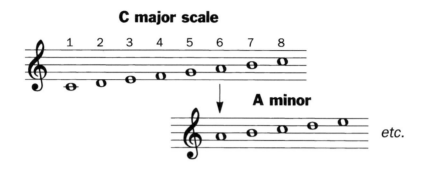

Therefore, A minor is the relative minor of C major - no ♭s or ♯s in the key signature.

Melodic minor scales

In the *ascending* scale, the 6th and 7th degrees are raised (sharpened) and in the *descending* scale they are lowered. (The descending scale of any melodic minor will have the same notes as its key signature.)

A melodic minor

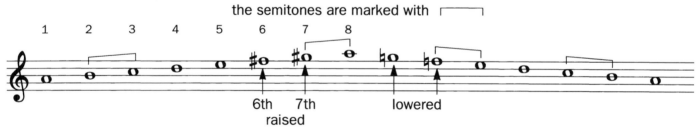

Harmonic minor scales

The notes of the harmonic minor scale are the same ascending *and* descending. The 7th degree is raised (sharpened). Notice the large gap of one and a half tones between degrees 6 and 7.

A harmonic minor

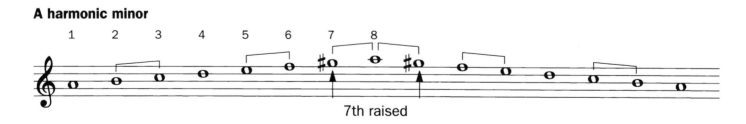

The tones and semitones of the first five degrees of both versions of the minor scale never change.

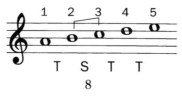

The sound of minor keys

The characteristic sound will tell you if the piece is in a major or a minor key. Minor keys are often used to express sad, sombre or mysterious moods.

1. *David of the White Rock* - (written here in A minor)   Welsh Air

2. *Pavane* (written here in A minor)   Fauré

3. Three themes from *Piano Concerto* in A minor - first movement   Grieg

Finding the relative minor

To find the relative minor of a major, count down three semitones from the key-note of the major.

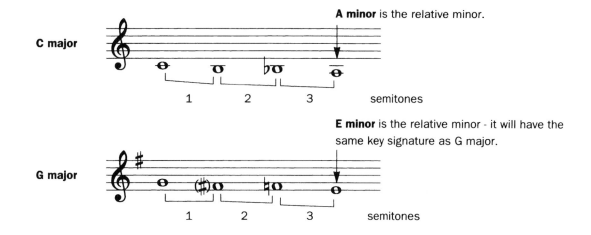

Look at page 68 (Book 2) - the *Gavotte* by Witthauer is in A minor.

9

Scale Study - A Minor

This study was written specifically for playing scale patterns - normally a melodic line would be based on the *melodic* version only.

C.B.

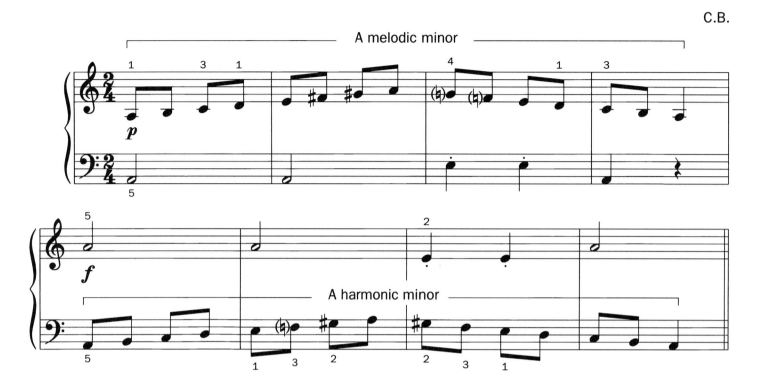

Major and minor scales with the same letter-name

C major and C minor are not related except that the scales use the same fingering. (They are sometimes called parallel scales.) The *third* degree of the minor scale with the same letter-name as the major scale, is always a semitone lower.

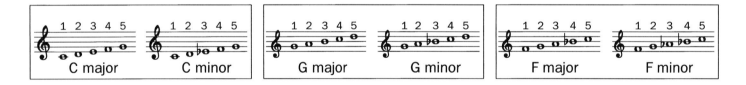

As you haven't learnt these minor scales, the key signatures have not been written in.

Au Clair de la Lune - French Folk Tune

Four bars in C major...

And now put into C minor.

10

Accidentals

When a ♯, ♭ or ♮ does not appear in the key signature but is written by the note each time it occurs, it is called an **accidental**. The accidentals in the piece below are mostly **G♯**s (the raised 7ths in the key of A minor). There is also a **C♯** in bar 15*. Don't forget that an accidental only changes later notes in the bar when they are on the *same* line or in the *same* space.

Look at *Teddington Blues* on page 72 (Book 2). It is in C major but has lots of accidentals which add 'spice'.

Waltz
in A minor

Moravian Folk Tune

*In bar 15, the third degree of the scale has been raised to **C♯**. Suddenly the piece has gone into A major.
Can you hear the change in mood?

11

E minor

E minor is the relative minor of G major, see page 99.

E melodic minor

6th 7th
raised
lowered

E harmonic minor

7th raised

Scale Study - E Minor

C.B.

E harmonic minor

E melodic minor

Sarabande
in E minor

Arcangelo Corelli (1653-1713)

Largo

mf

legato

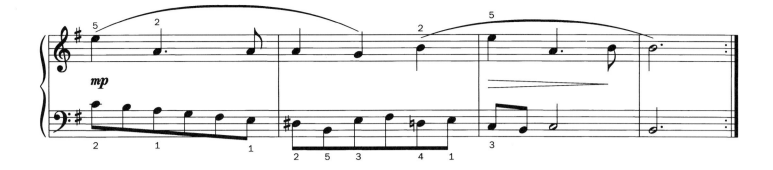

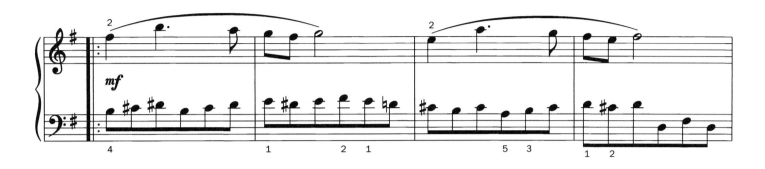

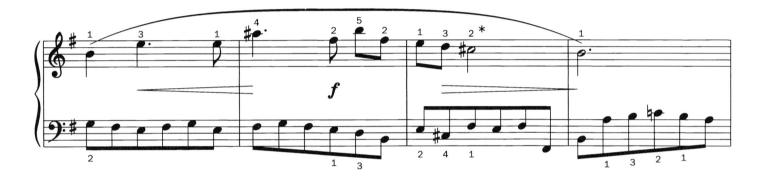

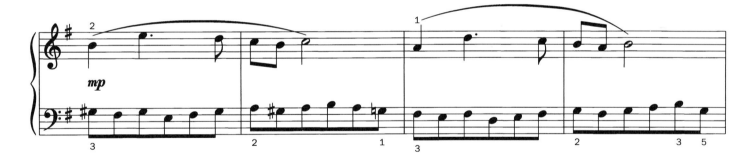

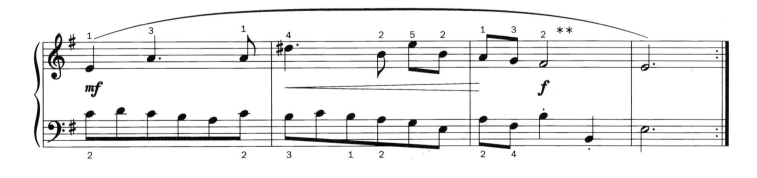

An excerpt from
First Loss

from *Album for the Young* (Op.68 No.16)

(This piece is in E minor)

Nicht schnell = not fast

fp = fortepiano = loud, then immediately soft

Nicht schnell ♩=96

Robert Schumann (1810-56)

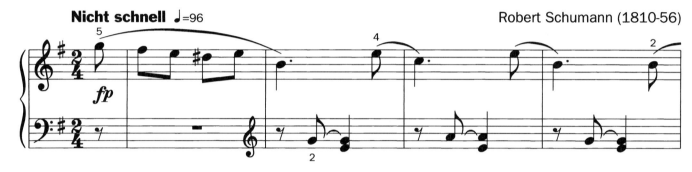

Fascinating snippet
'For years Schumann reigned a high authority on musical matters; but in an evil hour he fancied he could compose, and began, as he imagined, to exemplify his doctrines of taste by music of his own. Finding he could not follow in the path of the really great masters, he determined to strike out a new one for himself... The asylum at Düsseldorf can tell the sequel.' (H.F. Chorley, *Musical World*, London, 28 June 1856)

Tambourin

(in E minor)

The piece below is written in a typical eighteenth-century dance form with the drone bass giving the effect of a bagpipe (see Book 2, page 81).
This kind of piece was alternatively known as a Musette.

This wavy line is known as *Arpeggiando*. It tells you that the chord should be broken or spread, usually upwards, like a harp.

Adapted from
Jean-Philippe Rameau (1683-1764)

15

A new time signature

In $\frac{6}{8}$ time there are *two* main ♩. beats in each bar* and each beat is divided into *three* ♪s.

Think of $\frac{6}{8}$ as $\frac{2}{♩.}$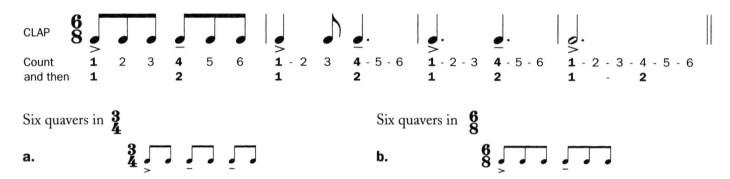

Count 6 at first to make it easy. Put an accent on the first count and a stress on the 4th.

CLAP	$\frac{6}{8}$																	
Count	1	2	3	4	5	6	1 - 2	3	4 - 5 - 6	1 - 2 - 3	4 - 5 - 6	1 - 2 - 3 - 4 - 5 - 6
and then	1			2			1		2	1	2	1 - 2

Six quavers in $\frac{3}{4}$

a. $\frac{3}{4}$

Six quavers in $\frac{6}{8}$

b. $\frac{6}{8}$

In **a.** and **b.** below, make sure that the speed of the quavers in both is the same.

a.

b.

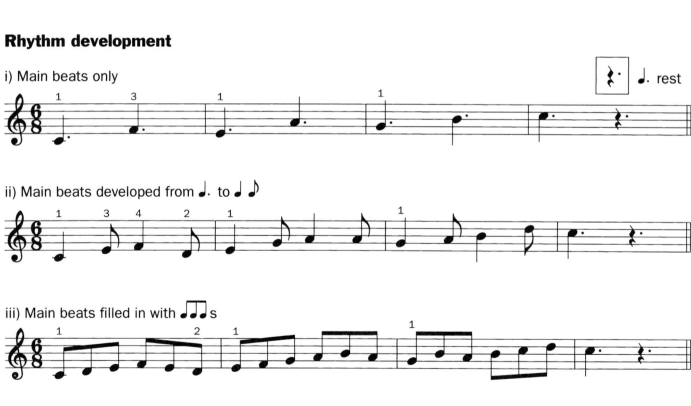

Rhythm development

i) Main beats only

⁣♩. rest

ii) Main beats developed from ♩. to ♩ ♪

iii) Main beats filled in with ♩♩♩s

*When the main beat is a *dotted* note as in $\frac{6}{8}$ this is known as *compound* time.

Two tunes in $\frac{6}{8}$

Lannagan's Ball

Irish Jig

If All the World were Paper

English Folk Tune

Four $\frac{6}{8}$ tunes by great composers

1. 'O, My Beloved Father' from *Gianni Schicchi*

Andante

Puccini

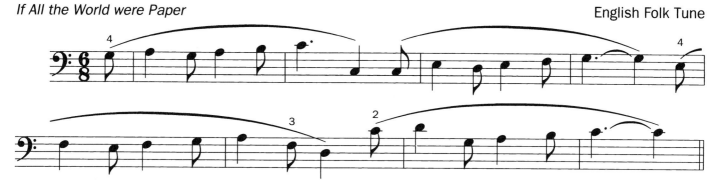

pp

2. Barcarolle from *The Tales of Hoffmann*

Moderato

Offenbach

mp

3. 'On Wings of Song'

Andante tranquillo

Mendelssohn

mp

4. Gigue from *Orchestral Suite No.3*

Allegro

J.S. Bach

mf

D minor

Relative minor of F major

Funeral March Of A Marionette

(in D minor)

Adapted from
Charles Gounod (1818-93)

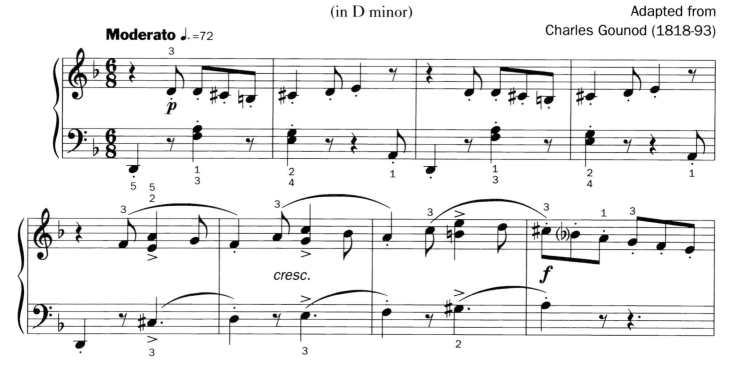

> **Fascinating snippet**
> You may recognise this tune. It became the signature tune of a
> very famous and lugubrious film director!

Theme from
Vltava
from *Má Vlast*

This theme is from a symphonic poem for orchestra
which describes the beauty of the River Moldau which
flows across Bohemia.

Adapted from
Bedřich Smetana (1824-84)

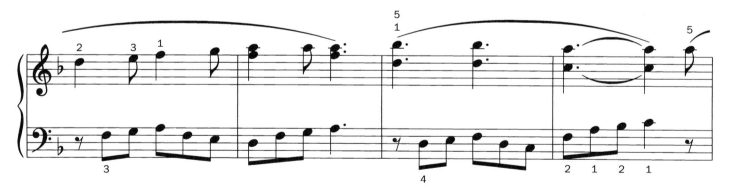

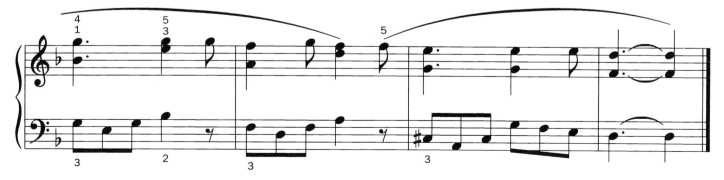

Fascinating snippet
Smetana's music drew upon all things Czech for its influence and
provided a stimulus to the strong feeling of nationalism which had
developed after the revolution of 1848.

Morning

from the *Peer Gynt Suite*

This orchestral suite was originally written to accompany Ibsen's play *Peer Gynt*.

New rhythm:

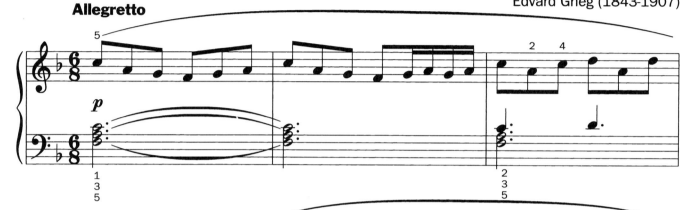

Adapted from
Edvard Grieg (1843-1907)

Fascinating snippet
The famous conductor Hans von Bülow called the Norwegian composer Grieg "the Chopin of the North".

20

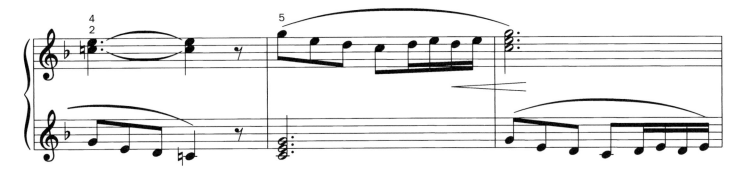

poco rit.   a tempo

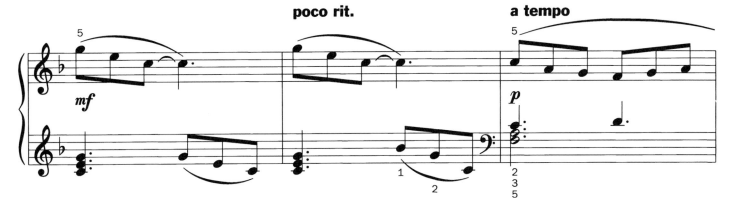

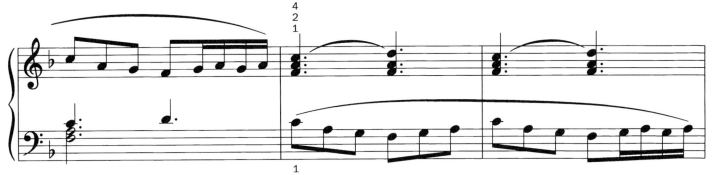

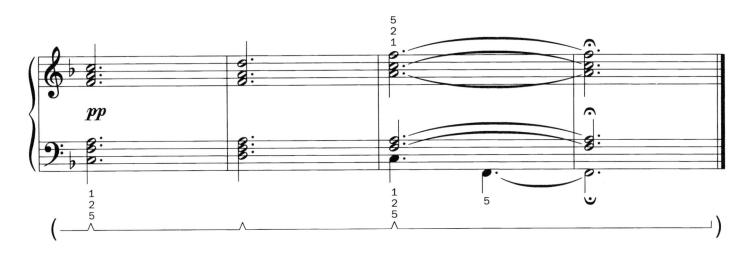

Dotted quavers in $\frac{6}{8}$

In the exercise below (two bars of *Blow the Man Down*), observe where the semiquavers in the right hand link up with the semiquavers in the left hand groups of six.

Exercise

Two tunes containing rhythms

1. 'The Flowers that Bloom in the Spring' from *The Mikado*

Sullivan

2. *Sicilienne*

Fauré

In what keys are the extracts above?

22

Greensleeves

English Air

Moderato

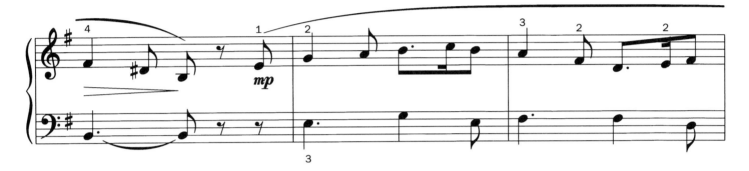

Suggested listening

Schubert's *Death and the Maiden* String Quartet in D minor,

last movement. This shows how exciting the rhythmic feel of $\frac{6}{8}$

can become.

Pick 'n' mix rhythms

These six rhythm exercises will work *together* - at the same time.

- The pupil and the teacher pick one exercise each from any of the six and then tap or clap them together.

- The pupil could record one (or even two) of the exercises, adding one 'live'.

- If you are in a group situation, everyone could pick an exercise and then the group can perform them all together. Make sure that someone counts as you clap, otherwise there's not much chance of you all keeping together! It may be easier if you count 6 ♪ s not 2 ♩. s as some of the rhythms are quite tricky.

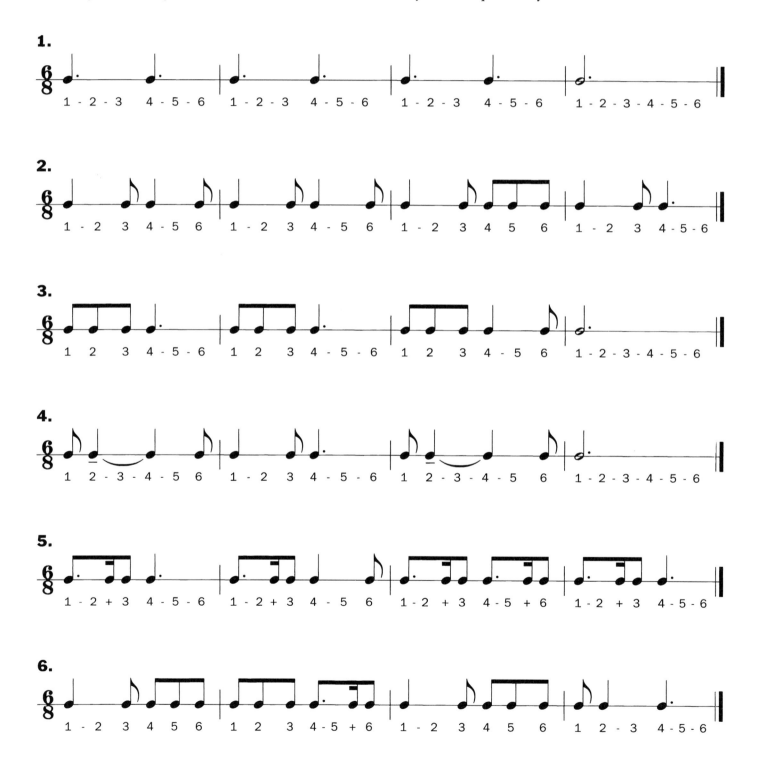

A new key signature

The key signature with two sharps is D major

 F# and C#

D major scale

German Dance

Allegro

Franz Joseph Haydn (1732-1809)

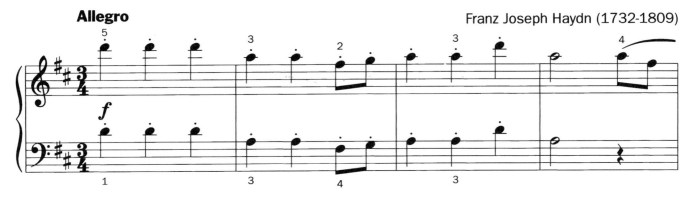

Intervals

An **interval** is the distance in pitch between two notes. To measure an interval, count the alphabet letter-names or the lines and spaces.

a 2nd   a 4th   a 3rd   a 5th

Harmonic interval

Melodic interval

When two notes are played together.

When two notes are played separately.

Triads

A **triad** is a chord of three notes and contains a root, 3rd and 5th.

5th
3rd
Root

When the notes of triads are played separately, they form broken chords and arpeggios.

Chord   Broken chords   An arpeggio

Primary chords (triads)

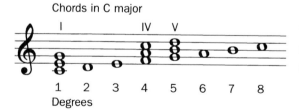

Chords in C major

I   IV V

1 2 3 4 5 6 7 8
Degrees

The chords on the 1st, 4th and 5th degrees of the scale are known as primary chords.

In 'classical' music they are denoted by Roman numerals or words - chord I (tonic), chord IV (subdominant) and chord V (dominant). The numerals refer to where the root occurs in the scale.

Fascinating snippet
Primary chords are to a musician what primary colours are to an artist.

Chord symbols

In 'popular' music, chord symbols are used e.g. the primary chords on page 116 are known as **C**, **F** and **G** - the letter-name of each root. Although every chord is *named* from the root, it can be *played* in different positions (inversions).

The chord of C

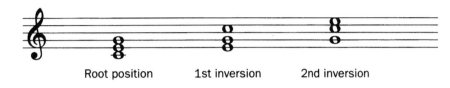

Root position   1st inversion   2nd inversion

Dominant 7th

The dominant 7th - V^7 - is built on the 5th (dominant) degree of the scale.

7th
5th
3rd
root

V^7 of C major

'Popular' chord symbols of V^7

Dominant 7th in C major = G^7
Dominant 7th in G major = D^7
Dominant 7th in F major = C^7

The root position of the dominant 7th above is rather clumsy to play and so it is usually played in other positions (inversions) e.g.

G^7 missing out the 5th.

Useful chord positions for harmonising simple tunes

The G major root positions and inversions below fall conveniently under the left hand.

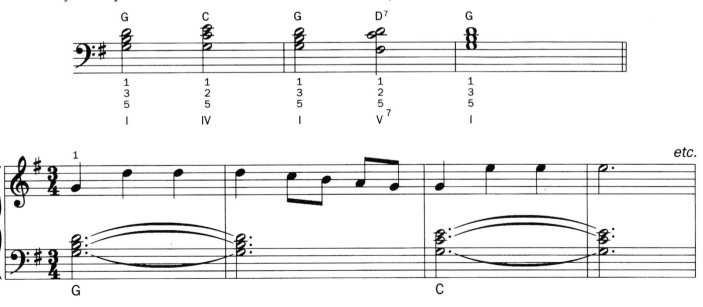

Some useful left-hand styles

i. *Broken chords*

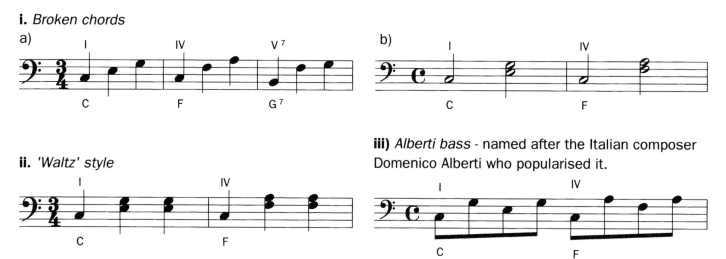

ii. *'Waltz' style*

iii) *Alberti bass* - named after the Italian composer Domenico Alberti who popularised it.

Mozart's use of the Alberti bass

Piano Sonata in C major

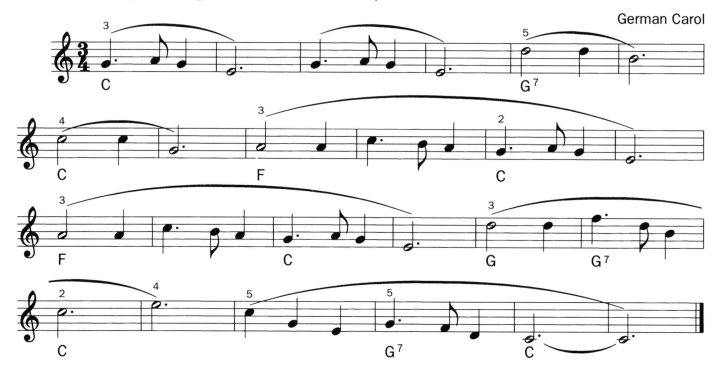

Allegro

etc.

D.I.Y. left hand

Silent Night

Add a left-hand part to the carol below using the chord symbols indicated. (Only change the chord when you see the next chord symbol.) Experiment with different bass styles.

German Carol

Suggested listening
First movement of Mozart's Piano Sonata in C K.545 (see above).

28

A new key signature

The key signature with two flats is B♭ major. $\begin{array}{c} \text{𝄢} \flat\flat \end{array}$ B♭ and E♭

Scale Study - B♭ Major

The fingering pattern in this study is different from previous major scales because the scale begins on a black note.

Theme fragment from

Variations On A Theme Of Haydn *
(St Anthony Chorale)

Caricature of Brahms on his way to the Hedgehog Inn.

MARY EVANS PICTURE LIBRARY

Fascinating snippet
The French composer Paul Dukas said of Brahms, "Too much beer and beard."

Adapted from
Johannes Brahms (1833-97)

Andante

p sostenuto

*See page 124 for Variations explanation.

29

Blues

The musical style called **'the blues'** is one of the earliest jazz forms and is based on a pattern - invariably a 12-bar pattern - using the three chords of I, IV and V.*

In its simplest form, this pattern is: 4 bars of I, 2 bars of IV, 2 bars of I, 1 bar of V, 1 bar of IV and 2 bars of I. (*Treadmill Blues* below follows this pattern.) The so-called *blue notes* that give this type of music its special 'feel' are the flattened 3rd, 5th and 7th notes of the scale. (**E♭**, **G♭** and **B♭** below - scale of C major.)

Treadmill Blues

Those of you using a digital piano could use the electric piano 'voice' for the pieces on pages 120 and 121.

* Later on in modern jazz, blues became more harmonically sophisticated although still adhering to a 12-bar pattern.

Frankie and Johnny

Here the 12-bar blues pattern is slightly altered to the following pattern:

4 bars of I, 3 bars of IV, 1 bar of I, 2 bars of V⁷, 2 bars of I.

Traditional American

More about time signatures

The beat is not always a crotchet (or, as in $\begin{smallmatrix}6\\8\end{smallmatrix}$ a dotted crotchet). Sometimes the beat is a minim as shown by the number 2 as the bottom number in the time signature. (The bottom number tells you the type of beat by its relationship to the semibreve e.g. there are 2 minims in a semibreve.)

$\begin{smallmatrix}4\\2\end{smallmatrix}$ = 4 minim beats in a bar

$\begin{smallmatrix}3\\2\end{smallmatrix}$ = 3 minim beats in a bar

$\begin{smallmatrix}3\\8\end{smallmatrix}$ = 3 quaver beats in a bar
(there are 8 quavers in a semibreve)

Sarabande

George Frideric Handel (1685-1759)

32

The Elephant

from *The Carnival of the Animals*

Count 1 2 3 1 2 + 3 + 1 2 3 1 - 2 3 1 + 2 3 | *etc.*

Adapted from
Camille Saint-Saëns (1835-1921)

Allegretto pomposo

sempre 8va bassa

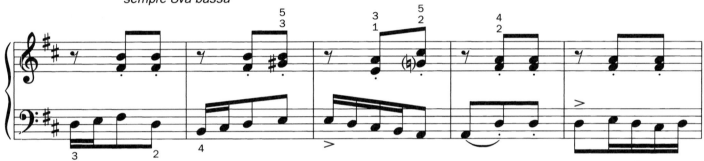

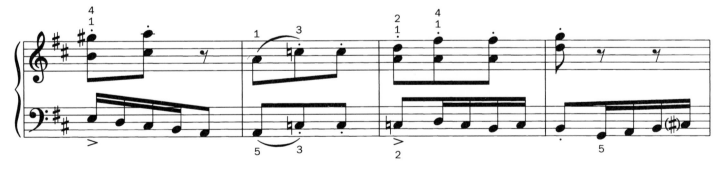

Theme and variations

A **variation** is a transformation of a theme which remains recognisable throughout. The theme may be transformed melodically and / or harmonically and / or rhythmically.

Theme and Variations K.265
on *Ah, vous dirai-je, maman?*

The theme and *one* variation are included here.

*Slip in the three small ornamental notes quickly before the main beat.

Fascinating snippet

Some sources attribute the melody of *Twinkle, Twinkle Little Star* to Mozart, who used it as the theme for his twelve keyboard variations K.265. Other sources believe it to be a favourite French nursery tune of the eighteenth century.

VARIATION

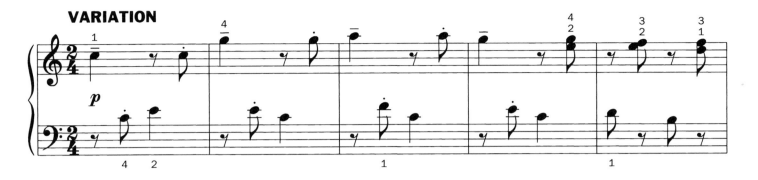

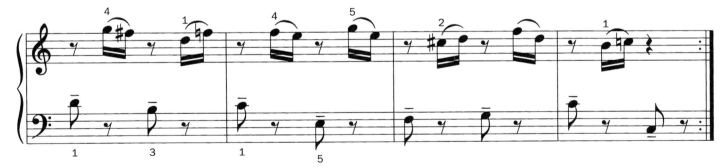

Suggested listening

Listen to K.265 in its complete form and to Dohnányi's *Variations on a Nursery Song* for piano and orchestra (1913). Beethoven wrote two sets of variations for cello and piano on themes from *The Magic Flute* by Mozart, Wo.046 and Op.66.

Theme from the
Unfinished Symphony

Suggested listening
Schubert's *Eighth Symphony* - the *'Unfinished'*.

Adapted from
Franz Schubert (1797-1828)

Trepak

from the ballet *The Nutcracker*

Fascinating snippet

'Tchaikovsky appears to be a victim of the epidemic of the Music of the Future, that in its hydrophobia, scorns logic, wallows in torpor, and time and again, collapses in dissonant convulsions...' (*Wiener Fremdenblatt*, 28 November 1876)

Adapted from

Peter Ilyich Tchaikovsky (1840-93)

Molto vivace

Dictionary of terms

used in Book 1

Presto = fast

Allegro = lively, quick

Moderato = moderately

Allegretto = fairly quick but not as quick as **Allegro**

Andante = at a medium pace

Andantino = slightly slower or faster than **Andante**

Adagio = slow

Lento = slow

Largo = very slow, stately

Andante con moto = at a medium pace but with movement
(**con** = with, **moto** = movement)

Ritardando
ritard. } = getting gradually slower
rit.

Ritenuto
riten. } = getting slower, held back
rit.

poco = a little

poco rit. = slow down a little

a tempo = in time, indicating a return to the original speed after e.g. rit.

grazioso = gracefully

con brio = with spirit

espressivo = expressively

simile = same as previously stated

used in Book 2

Larghetto = slow but not as slow as **Largo**

Vivace = lively, quick

Grave = very slow, solemn

Allargando = broadening out

con grazia = with grace

dolce = sweet, soft

giocoso = merry, playful

cantabile = in a singing style

used in Book 3

Nicht schnell = not fast

$\boldsymbol{fp}$ = **forte piano** = loud, then immediately soft

Well done!

You are now ready to tackle a wide range of repertoire including:

Tunes You've Always Wanted to Play

More Tunes You've Always Wanted to Play

by Carol Barratt

Also, look out for supplementary material in
The Classic Piano Collection

Fascinating snippet
Pavarotti, the famous Italian tenor, received 165 curtain calls and was applauded for one hour seven minutes after singing in Donizetti's 'L'elisir d'amore' in Berlin on 24 February 1988.

Keep practising!

Carol Barratt